Motorbike and Scooter learning through visualization.

Preface:

Knowledge is one of the most precious resources we can possess in life, and learning is a process that should never stop. In every field, learning is an endless journey, a path that requires curiosity, commitment, and perseverance.

This book aims to be a guide for those who wish to learn new disciplines and acquire new skills. In particular, it focuses on visualization as a learning tool. Visualization is a technique that allows creating mental images to represent ideas and concepts, helping to memorize and understand them better. Thanks to this technique, one can acquire deeper knowledge, learn faster, and develop a richer imagination.

The book is structured to offer a gradual path, starting from the basics of visualization and reaching more advanced techniques. It is a practical manual, rich in exercises and useful tips to improve one's visualization skills and apply them in different contexts.

I hope this book can be helpful to all those who want to deepen their knowledge and become true experts in the visualization technique. Enjoy reading!
As already described in my book 'The Right Way to Happiness' (available on Apple Books at the link https://books.apple.com/ch/book/la-via-giusta/id1562828084?l=it), some essential steps described can also be used in practical learning, particularly in driving a vehicle. If you have read the book, you may have noticed that some of these essential steps also reappear in this new book. The most important one relates to the abilities of our conscious mind. The term conscious refers to everything we are capable of doing simultaneously in the present. The book can be found on Amazon under the title 'The Right Way.' Creative visualization is a technique that involves imagining, or visualizing, things or situations in one's mind with the intention of manifesting them in reality. This spiritual technique is of fundamental importance in the teaching and practices of New Thought and positive thinking, and often accompanies the practice of positive affirmations or affirmative prayer. The proponents of the movement have theorized creative visualization since the end of the 19th century, and one of the first authors to talk about it was Wallace Wattles, author of 'The Science of Getting Rich.' The difference between creative visualization and daydreaming is that during the act of fantasizing, the person creates a mental image or scene of which they are an outside observer, while during the act of creative visualization, the person visualizing is at the very center of their visualization and experiences it firsthand, striving to perceive all the details through all the senses, in order to make it as real as possible.

Scholars have established that our conscious mind is capable of handling about seven elements simultaneously, while all the others are processed by our subconscious mind.

In modern psychology, the subconscious is defined as the part of the mind that records and maintains all information, concepts, images, and emotions, essentially everything that concerns us. The Conscious and the Subconscious do not necessarily correspond to everything we use and understand at this moment, but represent two different parts of our mind. The Conscious represents the part of our mind that deals with conscious activities such as attention, perception, short-term memory, and reasoning. The Subconscious, on the other hand, represents the part of our mind that deals with unconscious activities such as automatic processes, emotions, behaviors, and automatic thoughts.

In addition, the amount of information that our Conscious can handle can vary based on cognitive abilities and individual experience, but it is not limited to a precise number of elements. The ability to manage information can be improved with training and experience.

There are three steps to consider:

Use one element at a time, following an established order (for example, in a driving sequence, first look, then signal, then physically move the vehicle, and so on).
Repeat the elements until they become automatic, meaning they are handled by the subconscious.
Perform the exercise mentally, visualizing the movements and actions to be taken.
The first step involves using one element at a time, following the order from the first to the fifth. For example, to make a pre-selection, it is necessary to use the first 5 elements, and consequently, there are still 2 left.

The elements are: Signal Physically move the vehicle Slow down to search for the arrival point Reach the arrival point

The chapter deals with this topic and states that creative visualization can be useful for learning new skills. To support this thesis, reference is made to a study conducted more than 30 years ago in which three people were put in front of a computer screen to perform exercises. One person tried several times, another stopped after a few attempts, while the other turned off the computer and continued to do the exercise mentally. At the end of the test, it was found that the person who had done the exercise mentally had obtained the best results, demonstrating the effectiveness of mental exercise in practice. In the chapter on how to develop the sixth sense and also in the one on dreams, the element of visualization appears several times. Most people learn to drive through practice, as driving a vehicle represents a daily activity for many. However, the technique of creative visualization can be a valuable support for learning to drive. First, it is important to become familiar with the main driving techniques, which can be learned through specific courses, manuals or online tutorials. Then, it is possible to use creative visualization to improve the learning and memorization of driving techniques.

For example, you can mentally visualize the execution of specific maneuvers, such as parallel parking or entering a roundabout, imagining yourself driving the car and following all the phases of the maneuver. This way, you can learn the right sequences of actions to perform for each situation and memorize them more easily. It is also important to visualize particularly difficult driving situations, such as driving in rainy or foggy conditions, to mentally prepare for such situations and improve driving skills.

Remember that creative visualization cannot replace actual driving practice, but can be used as a valuable support to improve learning and driving safety. The first element that radically changes the approach to this new discipline, driving, is represented by the speed of the vehicle as it is higher than what we use for walking or running. We all know that our brain is programmed from birth for two speeds. To tackle curves on a two-wheeled vehicle, it is necessary to reduce speed in proportion to the radius of the curve. It is not possible to tackle a curve at the same speed reached on a straight road. In Europe, unless specific provisions are made by individual countries, speeds are 50 km/h in urban areas, 80 km/h or variable depending on the country outside urban areas, and 120 km/h or variable depending on the country on highways. These three speeds are also valid in the absence of specific signage. For all other speeds, road signs apply. In case of crossing a national border, you will find indications related to these three speeds at the customs. In the technique of curves for scooters and automatic motorcycles, the rear brake is located on the left, while the front brake is located on the right near the accelerator. Before tackling a curve, it's important to position yourself correctly by using both brakes (front and rear). It's necessary to have a complete view of the curve, considering its characteristics such as width and radius. Then, you must fix a trajectory that allows you to exit the curve with a constant speed. During the trajectory phase, it's fundamental to avoid using the front brake to not compromise the stability of the vehicle, while the rear brake can be used to slow down and stabilize the vehicle. Once the exit from the curve is identified, it's possible to accelerate and proceed towards the next positioning. Furthermore, it's important to maintain a space reserve of at least one meter towards the center of the road to avoid problems with oncoming traffic. Let's start with the technique of learning through visualization. As mentioned, you should treat each point separately and then connect them with the following points. Imagine the route with all the details, look for spaces to use as if you were in reality. Are you ready?

First Exercise: left turn.

Close your eyes and, while relaxed, mentally imagine the route you know. Imagine approaching the dynamic end point with a slowdown, then positioning yourself on the right side of the trajectory (corresponding to the right wheel of a four-wheeled vehicle). Repeat this exercise 5 times, always with your eyes closed. Have you done it? Now, still with your eyes closed, repeat the first exercise and add the search for the exit point.

Second Exercise: left turn.

Close your eyes and, while relaxed, mentally imagine the route you know. Visualize the starting trajectory (corresponding to the right wheel of a four-wheeled vehicle) and look for the exit point (corresponding to the left wheel of a four-wheeled vehicle). Repeat this exercise 5 times, always with your eyes closed. Have you done it? Now, still with your eyes closed, repeat the second exercise and add the execution of the route (trajectory) at the same speed.

Third Exercise: Left turn.

Close your eyes and, while relaxed, mentally imagine the path you know. Visualize the starting trajectory (corresponding to the right wheel of a four-wheeled vehicle), locate the exit point (corresponding to the left wheel of a four-wheeled vehicle), and then follow the path (trajectory) at the same speed. Repeat this exercise 5 times, always with your eyes closed. Did you do it? Now, still with your eyes closed, repeat the third exercise and add reaching the endpoint by increasing speed.

Fourth Exercise: Left turn.

Close your eyes and, while relaxed, mentally imagine the path you know:
Dynamic endpoint approaching with deceleration.
Locate the exit point.
Follow the path (trajectory) at the same speed.
Reach the endpoint by increasing speed. (Reserved space)*
Repeat this exercise 14 times with your eyes closed, visualizing each step in detail. In this way, your brain will automatically register these elements, without having to think about these 4 points again, while keeping the other 7 elements you used previously intact.

First Exercise: right turn.

Close your eyes and, in a relaxed state, mentally imagine a path that you know.
Dynamic endpoint approaching with deceleration, positioning the right turn trajectory on the left side (corresponding to the left wheel of a four-wheeled vehicle). Repeat this exercise 5 times with your eyes closed. Now, still with your eyes closed, repeat the first exercise and add searching for the exit point (right wheel of a four-wheeled vehicle).

Second Exercise: right turn.

Close your eyes and, in a relaxed state, mentally imagine a path that you know.
Dynamic endpoint approaching with deceleration, positioning the right turn trajectory on the left side (corresponding to the left wheel of a four-wheeled vehicle). Search for the exit point (right wheel of a four-wheeled vehicle). Repeat this exercise 5 times with your eyes closed.

Third Exercise: right turn.

Close your eyes and, in a relaxed state, mentally imagine a path that you know.
Dynamic endpoint approaching with deceleration, positioning the right turn trajectory on the left side (corresponding to the left wheel of a four-wheeled vehicle), search for the exit point (right wheel of a four-wheeled vehicle), perform the path (trajectory) at the same speed. Repeat this exercise 5 times with your eyes closed. Have you done it? Now, with your eyes still closed, repeat the third exercise and add reaching the endpoint (right wheel of a four-wheeled vehicle) while increasing the speed.

Fourth Exercise right turn.

Close your eyes and, while relaxing, mentally imagine a route you know. Approaching dynamic endpoint with slowing down, positioning right turn trajectory on the left side (corresponding to the left wheel of a four-wheeled vehicle), finding the exit point (right wheel of a four-wheeled vehicle), performing the trajectory at the same speed, reaching the endpoint (right wheel of a four-wheeled vehicle) while increasing the speed. Repeat this exercise 5 times with your eyes closed. Have you done it? Now, make this right turn automatic. Close your eyes, visualize the road where you are doing the exercise, and repeat it 14 times. Are you ready? Let's do it: 1 Positioning: approaching dynamic endpoint with slowing down. (Reserved space)* 2 Finding the exit point. 3 Performing the trajectory at the same speed. 4 Reaching the endpoint (right wheel of a four-wheeled vehicle) while increasing the speed.

Your brain has recorded everything so that you don't have to think about these 4 elements anymore while keeping intact the 7 elements used by your consciousness. Try driving on the road and you will see that curves will no longer be a problem for you. Drive safely in traffic. In order to drive safely in traffic, it's important to follow some basic rules: Use space effectively, avoiding only looking at obstacles but also observing oncoming traffic. Maintain a safe distance from the vehicle in front, keeping at least 2 seconds of distance. This can help avoid accidents and ensure smoother driving. Respect speed limits and adjust speed to the flow of traffic. It's important to pay attention to road signs and drive responsibly. When there are multiple options on the road, such as in the presence of an emergency lane or a lane reserved for public transportation, it's important to pre-select to the right to leave space for bicycles, scooters and other non-motorized vehicles. Instead, when driving on a one-way street, it can be useful to move completely to the left to promote traffic flow. Remember that driving in traffic requires attention, caution and respect for road rules to ensure the safety of all road users.

Pre-selection to the right:

Firstly, it is necessary to make it possible to turn right without a bicycle, scooter, or other vehicle passing by during the maneuver. To do this, it is important to look and signal your intention, using the central and side rearview mirrors to check the situation behind your vehicle and to the right, checking the space on the right by turning your head 90 degrees. If there are no bicycles or other obstacles, you can close the space by moving the vehicle to the right about 5 meters before turning. During the right turn, it is important to avoid ending up in the opposite direction. To do this, it is necessary to know where to position oneself on the road. After making the move to close the space, it is necessary to slow down the vehicle and look for the arrival point on the right. Once the arrival point has been identified, you can reach it at the same speed.

Pre-selection to the left:

As in the pre-selection to the right (Look and signal, use the right side mirror to see the situation behind our vehicle from afar, use the left side mirror to see behind on the left if there are vehicles approaching, check the space on the left by turning your head 90 degrees), if the space is free, make the move to the left without crossing the safety line marking the road, about 5 meters before the intersection. Continuing, after creating a trajectory that avoids invading the opposite lane, slow down to look for the arrival point. To make this operation possible, it is necessary to establish the exact curved line that our vehicle must follow by looking for the arrival point. Before turning, it will be necessary to check that the space in the opposite direction (traffic in the opposite direction) is sufficient to make the left turn possible. When in doubt, wait.

Exercise Right-hand preselection:

Close your eyes and, while relaxed, mentally repeat. Ready, set, go: Look at the left rearview mirror to check the situation behind your vehicle. Look at the right rearview mirror to check the situation on the right side of your vehicle. Turn your head 90 degrees to the right to check the situation on the right side of your vehicle. Activate the turn signal to signal your intention to turn right. Move the vehicle to the right about 5 meters before the intersection to prevent bicycles and other vehicles from passing by. Slow down the vehicle to search for the destination point and reach it while maintaining the same speed. Mentally repeat this exercise five times, imagining yourself driving the vehicle.

Exercise Left-hand preselection:

Close your eyes and, while relaxed, mentally repeat. Ready, set, go:
Look at the right rearview mirror to check the situation behind your vehicle.
Turn your head 90 degrees to the left to check the situation on the left side of your vehicle.
Move the vehicle to the left without crossing the safety line, about 5 meters before the intersection.

Continue by creating a trajectory that avoids invading the opposite lane.
Slow down the vehicle to search for the destination point and establish the exact curved line that the vehicle must follow.
Check that the space on the opposite lane is sufficient to make the left turn, in case of doubt, wait.
Make a left turn following the predetermined trajectory.
Mentally repeat this exercise five times, imagining yourself driving the vehicle.

Third right pre-selection exercise.

Ready, set, go: Left rearview mirror, right rearview mirror, turn head 90 degrees to the right, turn on signal, move to the right. Repeat this exercise 5 times with your eyes closed. Did you do it?
Now, still with your eyes closed, repeat the third exercise and add slowing down.

Fourth right pre-selection exercise.

Ready, set, go: Left rearview mirror, right rearview mirror, turn head 90 degrees to the right, turn on signal, move to the right, slow down. Repeat this exercise 5 times with your eyes closed. Did you do it? Now, still with your eyes closed, repeat the fourth exercise and add searching for the arrival point on the road.

Fifth right pre-selection exercise.

Ready, set, go: Left rearview mirror, right rearview mirror, turn head 90 degrees to the right, turn on signal, move to the right, slow down, search for the arrival point on the road. Repeat this exercise 5 times with your eyes closed. Did you do it? Now that you have memorized the different steps, imagine a road that you know well and visually perform the five exercises. Did you do it?
You will have noticed that the sequence of 5 steps was carried out without problems. Let's now perform this step automatically: Close your eyes and visualize the road where you will perform the exercise. Mentally repeat the following 7 elements 14 times: left rearview mirror right rearview mirror turn your head 90 degrees left turn signal close the gap slow down destination point Now you are ready. Your brain has recorded these elements automatically, so you no longer have to think about them. Try to go on the road and you will see how left lane changes will no longer be a problem for you.

First exercise: left lane change in a one-way street.

Close your eyes and relax. Mentally visualize the exercise elements and repeat it 5 times with your eyes closed: left rearview mirror, right rearview mirror, turn your head 90 degrees.
Now, with your eyes still closed, repeat the first exercise and add the left turn signal.

Second exercise:

Ready, set, go: right rearview mirror, left rearview mirror, turn your head 90 degrees, left turn signal. Repeat this exercise 5 times with your eyes closed.
Now, with your eyes still closed, repeat the second exercise and add the leftward movement of the vehicle to promote traffic flow.

Third exercise:

Ready, set, go: check the right rearview mirror, check the left rearview mirror, turn your head 90 degrees, signal left, move flush with the center safety line or, if there isn't one, stay in the middle of the road leaving space for oncoming traffic. Repeat this exercise 5 times with your eyes closed. Now, with your eyes still closed, repeat the third exercise and add in slowing down.

Fourth exercise:

Ready, set, go: check the right rearview mirror, check the left rearview mirror, turn your head 90 degrees, signal left, move flush with the center safety line or, if there isn't one, stay in the middle of the road leaving space for oncoming traffic, slow down. Repeat this exercise 5 times with your eyes closed. Now, with your eyes still closed, repeat the fourth exercise and add in searching for the lane of the destination point. Imagine a curved line that starts when your vehicle is halfway across the roadway or, in a one-way street, at the beginning of the edge of the new road.

Fifth exercise:

Ready, set, go: check the right rearview mirror, check the left rearview mirror, turn your head 90 degrees, signal left, move flush with the center safety line or, if there isn't one, stay in the middle of the road leaving space for oncoming traffic, slow down, search for the lane of the destination point. Imagine a curved line that starts when your vehicle is halfway across the roadway or, in a one-way street, at the beginning of the edge of the new road. Repeat this exercise 5 times with your eyes closed.

Make the left automatic preselection.

Let's do it: Close your eyes and visualize the road where you will do the exercise. Repeat the following steps mentally 14 times. Are you ready? Let's go: Right rearview mirror, left rearview mirror, turn your head 90 degrees. Left turn signal. Move over. Slow down. Look for the endpoint. Your brain has recorded everything so that you no longer have to focus on these 5 elements, while still keeping the 7 elements used by your conscious mind unchanged. Try going on the road and you will see how left automatic preselection will no longer be a problem for you. Approach technique for roundabouts, right-of-way, and yielding. In all these cases, you should approach with a speed that allows you to have 3 options: Continue driving, or better yet, continue on. Slow down and continue on. Stop.

Let's examine the three options in roundabouts:

Proceeding (option 1) is used when, having enough space on my left, I can go towards the endpoint that I had previously set. The space is the one that goes from my entrance to the entrance before mine. Verify the space by turning your head to the left for a duration of 0.25 seconds (glance). The endpoint corresponds to the exact point where my vehicle must go. The information related to the endpoint is registered in our brain for about 3 seconds, while the free space on the left for only 0.25 seconds. Slowing down and proceeding (option 2) is used when we find a space on the left that, although occupied, becomes free, creating the possibility to continue towards the endpoint that I had previously set. The space is the one that goes from my entrance to the entrance before mine. Verify the space by turning your head to the left by 45 degrees for a duration of 0.25 seconds (glance), evaluating the free space that is created by the vehicle that is occupying that space by freeing it. When in doubt, stop. The endpoint corresponds to the exact point where my vehicle must go. The information related to the endpoint is registered in our brain for about 3 seconds, while the free space on the left for only 0.25 seconds. Stopping (option 3) when the space on your left is occupied and does not become free immediately. Let's start with the technique of learning through visualization for the roundabout. As mentioned before, you have to treat each point separately and then connect them with the other subsequent points. Imagine the route with all the details, look for the spaces to use as if you were in reality. Are you ready?

First exercise for the roundabout:

Close your eyes and, well relaxed, mentally imagine adjusting the approach speed in such a way as to have the three options: go, slow down and stop. Repeat this exercise 5 times, always with your eyes closed. Have you finished? Now, still with your eyes closed, repeat the first exercise and add the search for the endpoint.

Second exercise for the roundabout:

Close your eyes and, while being relaxed, mentally imagine adjusting your approach speed to have the three options: go, slow down, and stop, and look for the point of arrival. Repeat this exercise 5 times, always with your eyes closed. Are you done? Now, still with your eyes closed, repeat the second exercise and add the search for space on your left side, turning your head 45 degrees inside the roundabout. The search should take place just before entering the roundabout to make all three options possible, including stopping.

Third exercise for the roundabout:

Close your eyes and, while being relaxed, mentally imagine adjusting your approach speed to have the three options: go, slow down, and stop, look for the point of arrival, and search for space on your left side by turning your head 45 degrees inside the roundabout with a glance of 0.25 seconds. Repeat this exercise 5 times, always with your eyes closed. Are you done? Now, still with your eyes closed, repeat the third exercise and add reaching the previously sought point of arrival if the space allows it. After doing the first exercise for 5 times, make 2 passes: the second with the space that frees up to slow down and go, and the third with no space to stop.

Fourth exercise for the roundabout:

Adjust your approach speed to have the three options: go, slow down, and stop, look for the point of arrival, search for space on your left side by turning your head 45 degrees inside the roundabout with a glance of 0.25 seconds, and go to the previously sought point of arrival. Repeat this exercise 5 times, always with your eyes closed.

Repeat the exercise for the second option, slowing down and going.

Adjust the approach speed in a way that gives you the 3 options, which are to go, slow down and go, stop, look for the arrival point, search for space on your left by turning your head 45 degrees inside the roundabout with a glance of 0.25 seconds, and wait that tenth of a second for the space to free up and go to the arrival point. Repeat this exercise 5 times always with your eyes closed. Have you done it?

Repeat the exercise for the third option, stopping.

Adjust the approach speed in a way that gives you the 3 options, which are to go, slow down and go, stop, look for the arrival point, search for space on your left by turning your head 45 degrees inside the roundabout with a glance of 0.25 seconds and stop, waiting for the space to free up. Search for the arrival point again and when space allows, go there. Repeat this exercise 5 times always with your eyes closed. Have you done it?

Now, still with your eyes closed, repeat the fourth exercise and add the search for the arrival point about 5 meters outside the roundabout.

Fifth Exercise for the roundabout

Ready, set, go: Adjust your approach speed so that it gives you the 3 options, namely to go slow and go, stop, look for the arrival point, search for the space on your left by turning your head 45 degrees inside the roundabout with a glance of 0.25 seconds and go to the previously searched arrival point, add the new arrival point outside about 5 meters from the roundabout. Repeat this exercise 5 times always with your eyes closed. Have you done it? If you wish, you can integrate the two variants Slow down and go and Stop, by repeating the two exercises of the fourth exercise with the addition of searching for the arrival point about 5 meters outside the roundabout. Now, still with your eyes closed, repeat the fifth exercise and add turning your head 90 degrees to the right to check for free space before exiting.

Sixth Exercise for the roundabout

Ready, set, go: Adjust your approach speed so that it gives you the 3 options, namely to go slow and go, stop, look for the arrival point, search for the space on your left by turning your head 45 degrees inside the roundabout with a glance of 0.25 seconds and go to the previously searched arrival point, add the new arrival point outside about 5 meters from the roundabout, and turn your head 90 degrees to the right to check for free space before exiting. Repeat this exercise 5 times always with your eyes closed. Have you done it? Now, still with your eyes closed, repeat the sixth exercise and add the right turn signal to go to the point of arrival outside the roundabout.

Seventh Exercise for the roundabout

Ready, set, go: Adjust the approach speed so that it gives you the 3 possibilities, i.e. go slow down and go, stop, look for the point of arrival, search for the space on your left by turning your head 45 degrees inside the roundabout with a glance of 0.25 seconds and go to the previously sought after point of arrival, add the new point of arrival about 5 meters outside the roundabout, turn your head 90 degrees to the right to check the free space before exiting, add the right turn signal to go to the point of arrival outside the roundabout. Repeat this exercise 5 times always with your eyes closed. Have you done it?" Automating the roundabout exercise can be helpful in improving your driving skills and making the driving experience less stressful. Here's how to do it: Before entering the roundabout, adjust your approach speed. Look for the desired point of arrival inside the roundabout. Check the space on your left and head towards the previously identified point of arrival. Once you reach the point of arrival, look for a new point of arrival inside the roundabout. Check the free space again before exiting the roundabout. If necessary, use the right turn signal to indicate your intention to exit the roundabout. Repeat these steps 14 times, visualizing the road where you will do the exercise. This way, your brain will record the process automatically, and you won't have to consciously think about each individual element. Once you are ready, try to perform the exercise on the road, and you will notice how the roundabout will no longer be a problem for you. For multi-lane roundabouts, the same technique of giving way and following the mandatory direction applies. However, we will delve into this topic in the chapter dedicated to driving in multi-lane roundabouts at the end of this book.

Giving way to the right applies everywhere.

To know if there is a giving way to the right, you need to observe the lane on the right and look for the pavement that re-enters on the right. If you find it, there is probably a giving way to the right. Giving way to the right means that vehicles coming from the right have priority over us. The priority situation occurs when two vehicles should continue at the same speed, and there would be a risk of collision. There are three options for giving way to the right:

Go: it is used when there is enough space on the right to continue towards the predetermined point of arrival. The available space goes from our position to the right inside the road for about 5 meters. The availability of space is checked by turning the head to the right by 45 degrees for 0.25 seconds (glance). If the space is clear, you can proceed at the established speed.

Slow down and go: it is used when the space on the right is occupied but immediately freed by the vehicle coming from the right. In this case, you must slow down and wait for the space to free up to proceed. The availability of space is checked as in the previous case, by turning the head to the right by 45 degrees for 0.25 seconds. If the space is clear, you can proceed at the speed created after slowing down.

Stop:

it is used when the space on the right is occupied, and you cannot proceed. In this case, you must stop and wait for the space to free up to resume driving towards the predetermined point of arrival. The availability of space is checked as in the previous cases, by turning the head to the right by 45 degrees for 0.25 seconds. If the space is clear, you can resume driving. Now let's start with the visualization learning technique for right-of-way. As mentioned, you have to treat each point separately and then connect it with the next points. Imagine the path with all the details, look for spaces to use as if you were in reality. Are you ready?

Right-of-Way

First Exercise Right-of-Way:

Ready, set, go! Close your eyes and, relaxed, mentally imagine adjusting your approach speed to give you the 3 options, that is, to go, slow down and stop. Repeat this exercise 5 times always with your eyes closed. Done?

Now, still with your eyes closed, repeat the first exercise and add the search for the arrival point about 5 meters in front of you.

Second Exercise Right-of-Way:

Ready, set, go! Close your eyes and, relaxed, mentally imagine adjusting your approach speed to give you the 3 options, that is, to go, slow down and stop, and look for the arrival point. Repeat this exercise 5 times always with your eyes closed. Done?

Now, still with your eyes closed, repeat the second exercise and add the search for space on your right by turning your head 45 degrees to the right. The search for space must take place just before the road on the right to make the 3 options possible, including stopping.

Third Exercise Right-of-Way:

Ready, set, go! Close your eyes and, relaxed, mentally imagine adjusting your approach speed to give you the 3 options, that is, to go, slow down and stop, look for the arrival point and search for space on your right by turning your head 45 degrees with a glance of 0.25 seconds. Repeat this exercise 5 times always with your eyes closed. Done?

Now let's begin with the visualization learning technique for right-of-way. As mentioned, you have to treat each point separately and then connect it with the following points. Imagine the path with all the details, search for spaces to use as if you were in reality. Are you ready?

Right-of-Way Exercise One:

Ready, set, go! Close your eyes and, while relaxed, mentally imagine adjusting your approach speed in a way that gives you three options, i.e., go, slow down, and stop. Repeat this exercise five times with your eyes closed. Done? Now, still with your eyes closed, repeat the first exercise and add the search for the destination point about 5 meters ahead of you. Right-of-Way Exercise Two: Ready, set, go! Close your eyes and, while relaxed, mentally imagine adjusting your approach speed in a way that gives you three options, i.e., go, slow down, and stop, and search for the destination point. Repeat this exercise five times with your eyes closed. Done? Now, still with your eyes closed, repeat the second exercise and add the search for space on your right by turning your head 45 degrees to the right. The search for space should occur just before the road on the right to make the three options possible, including stopping.

Right-of-Way Exercise Three:

Ready, set, go! Close your eyes and, while relaxed, mentally imagine adjusting your approach speed in a way that gives you three options, i.e., go, slow down, and stop, search for the destination point and search for space on your right by turning your head 45 degrees with a glance of 0.25 seconds. Repeat this exercise five times with your eyes closed. Done? Now, still with your eyes closed, repeat the third exercise and add reaching the destination point if space allows. After doing the first exercise five times, do two passes: the second with space clearing (slowing down and going) and the third with nonexistent space (stopping). Right-of-Way Exercise Four: Ready, set, go! Close your eyes and, while relaxed, mentally imagine adjusting your approach speed in a way that gives you three options, i.e., go, slow down, and stop. Search for the destination point and search for space on your right by turning your head 45 degrees with a glance of 0.25 seconds. Reach the destination point if space allows. After doing this exercise five times, do two passes: the second with space clearing, slowing down and going, and the third with nonexistent space, stopping. Repeat this exercise five times with your eyes closed. Done?

Making the right-of-way exercise automatic. Let's do it.

Close your eyes and visualize the road where you are doing the exercise and repeat it 14 times. Are you ready? Ready, set, go: Adjust your approach speed. Search for the destination point. Search for space on your right by turning your head 45 degrees. Reach the destination point. Your brain has recorded everything in such a way that you no longer have to think about these four elements, keeping the seven elements used by your consciousness intact. Try going on the road and you will see how the right-of-way will no longer be a problem for you."

Give right-of-way to straight traffic.

Let's see the three options for giving way. The space in meters is indicative and may vary depending on the speed. Go: it is used when, having sufficient space on my right and left, I can continue towards the destination point that I had set previously. The space is that which goes from my position to the left and to the right for about 5 meters in both directions. The space is checked by turning my head to the right at a 45-degree angle for a duration of 0.25 seconds in both directions. If the spaces are free, I continue at the speed that I had set, approaching the same. Slow down and go: it is used when, the spaces being occupied, but immediately freed by the vehicles on my left and right, I can continue after having slowed down sufficiently so that the spaces are free again, to continue towards the destination point that I had set previously. The space is that which goes from my position to the left and right inside the roads that I find on the left and right for about 5 meters. The space is checked by turning my head to the right at a 45-degree angle for a duration of 0.25 seconds in both directions. If the space or spaces are free, I continue at the speed that has been created after the slowdown.

Stop:

"Stop" is used when, the space or spaces being occupied by vehicles on my right or left, I cannot continue. To continue, I must, when the space is free, look for the destination point again and repeat the whole operation. The space is that which goes from my position to the right or left for about 5 meters. The space is checked by turning my head to the right at a 45-degree angle for a duration of 0.25 seconds in both directions (glance). If the space or spaces are free, I continue. Now let's start with the visualization learning technique to give way straight ahead. As mentioned, you need to treat each point separately and then connect it with the following points. Imagine the route with all the details, search for the spaces to use as if you were in reality. Are you ready?

First Exercise for giving way straight ahead:

On your marks, get set, go! Close your eyes and, while relaxing, mentally imagine: Adjusting your approach speed so that it gives you the 3 possibilities, i.e. go, slow down and stop. Repeat this exercise 5 times always with your eyes closed. Have you done it? Now, still with your eyes closed, repeat the first exercise and add the search for the destination point about 5 meters ahead of you.

Second Exercise for giving way straight ahead:

On your marks, get set, go! Close your eyes and, while relaxing, mentally imagine:Adjusting your approach speed so that it gives you the 3 possibilities, i.e. go, slow down and stop, searching for the destination point. Repeat this exercise 5 times always with your eyes closed. Have you done it? Now, still with your eyes closed, repeat the second exercise and add the search for the space on your left and right by turning your head 45 degrees in both directions. The space search should take place just before the road on the left and right to make the 3 variants possible, including stopping.

Third Exercise for giving way straight ahead:

On your marks, get set, go! Close your eyes and, while relaxing, mentally imagine:
Adjusting your approach speed so that it gives you the 3 possibilities, i.e. go, slow down and stop, searching for the destination point, searching for the space on your left and right by turning your head 45 degrees in both directions with a glance of 0.25 seconds. Repeat this exercise 5 times always with your eyes closed.

Make giving priority on the right automatic. Close your eyes and visualize the road where you want to practice. Repeat the following steps mentally 14 times. Are you ready? Starting point: Adjust your approach speed. Look for the arrival point on your right. Turn your head 45 degrees to the left and identify the available space for your maneuver on the left. Reach the arrival point on your right. Your brain has memorized these four steps in such a way that you won't have to think about them anymore, allowing you to focus on the other seven elements used by your consciousness. Now, go on the road and you will notice how giving priority on the right will no longer be a problem for you. To give priority by turning right, you have the following options. The space in meters is indicative and may vary depending on the speed.

Option 1

- Go: Use this option when you have enough space on your left to continue towards the previously established arrival point. The available space extends from your position to the left for about 5 meters. Check the space by turning your head to the left 45 degrees for 0.25 seconds. If the space is clear, proceed at the established speed after slowing down.

Option 2

- Slow down and go: Use this option when the space on your left is occupied, but will be immediately freed up by the vehicle occupying it. Slow down enough to allow the necessary space for your maneuver and proceed towards the previously established arrival point. The available space extends from your position to the left inside the left-hand side of the road for about 5 meters. Check the space by turning your head to the left 45 degrees for 0.25 seconds. If the space is clear, proceed at the established speed after slowing down.

Option 3

- Stop: Use this option when the space on your left is occupied and you cannot continue. To resume the maneuver, you will have to wait for the space to clear and repeat the entire procedure. The available space extends from your position to the left for about 5 meters. Check the space by turning your head to the left 45 degrees for 0.25 seconds. If the space is occupied, stop. If the space has just been freed up, you can proceed. If the space is clear, proceed.

Now, let's start with the visualization learning technique for giving priority by turning right.

Fifth exercise turning right.

Here we go: Close your eyes and, while relaxed, mentally imagine: regulate your approach speed so that you have the 3 options, i.e. to go, to slow down and to stop, check the left and right rear-view mirrors, turn your head 90 degrees, move to the right to close the gap for the cyclists, about 5 meters before giving way, slow down to look for the arrival point, and look for it on your right. Repeat this exercise 5 times with your eyes closed. Have you done it?

Now that you have performed these exercises mentally, I recommend that you repeat the same exercises on the road, always paying close attention to road safety and respecting traffic rules. In this way, you can acquire greater awareness of your driving skills and improve your performance on the road.

Fifth exercise: turning right.

Ready, set, go: Close your eyes and, while relaxed, mentally imagine adjusting your approach speed to give you three options: go, slow down, and stop. Then, use the left and right rearview mirrors, turn your head 90 degrees to look behind you, and move to the right to close the gap for cyclists, about 5 meters before giving way. Slow down to find the destination point on your right and locate it with a quick glance (0.25 seconds), while at the same time checking the space on your left. Repeat this exercise 5 times, always with your eyes closed. Now, still with your eyes closed, repeat the sixth exercise and add: if the space on your right for about 5 meters is clear, reach the destination point on your right by turning the steering wheel at the height of the beginning of the road mirror. Repeat this exercise 5 times, always with your eyes closed. Finally, repeat the seventh exercise: adjust your approach speed, use the rearview mirrors, turn your head 90 degrees, move to the right to close the gap for cyclists, slow down to find the destination point on your right, locate it with a quick glance, check the space on your left, and if the space on your right for about 5 meters is clear, reach the destination point by turning the steering wheel at the height of the beginning of the road mirror. Repeat this exercise 5 times, always with your eyes closed. Have you done it?

Making the exercise of giving way while turning right automatic.

Let's do it: Close your eyes and mentally visualize the road on which you are doing the exercise. Repeat this visualization 14 times. Are you ready? Let's start: Adjust your approach speed. Left rearview mirror, right rearview mirror, turn your head 90 degrees. Move to the right. Slow down. Look for the arrival point on your right. Look for space on your left. Reach the arrival point. Your brain has recorded these steps in such a way that you won't have to think about them in the future, keeping the information intact in your consciousness. Try it on the road and you will see how giving way by turning right will no longer be a problem for you. Giving way by turning left: The options are the same as giving way by turning right. The space in meters is indicative and may vary depending on the speed.

"Go"

is used when, having sufficient space on your right and left and in front (oncoming traffic), you can proceed towards the arrival point you had previously set. The space extends for about 5 meters to the left and right of your position. To check the space, turn your head to the right at a 45-degree angle for a duration of 0.25 seconds in both directions (glance). If the spaces are free, you can proceed at the speed you had set, approaching the arrival point.

"Slow down and go"

is used when, although the spaces are occupied, they are immediately vacated by the vehicles on your right and left and in front (opposing traffic), and you can proceed after slowing down sufficiently for the spaces to be free again, and then proceed towards the destination point that you had previously set. The space extends about 5 meters to your left and right within the road that you find on your left, right, and in front (opposing traffic). To check the space, turn your head 45 degrees to the right for a duration of 0.25 seconds in both directions (glance). If the spaces are free, you can proceed at the speed that was created after slowing down.

"Stop"

is used when the spaces are occupied by vehicles on your right or left and in front (opposing traffic), and you cannot proceed. To proceed, when the space clears, you will have to search for the destination point again and repeat the entire operation. The space is the one that extends from my position to the right or left, and in front (opposing traffic), for about 5 meters. You can check the space by turning your head to the right and left 45 degrees for a duration of 0.25 seconds (glance) in both directions and in front (opposing traffic).

Now let's start with the visualization learning technique for giving way by turning left. As mentioned, you should treat each point separately and then connect it with the other subsequent points. Imagine the route with all the details and search for the spaces to use as if you were in reality.
Are you ready?

First exercise: give way by turning left.

Ready, set, go! Close your eyes and, while staying relaxed, mentally imagine adjusting your approach speed to have three options: go straight, slow down or stop. Repeat this exercise 5 times with your eyes closed. Done? Now, still with your eyes closed, repeat the first exercise and add the left preselection using the right and left rearview mirrors and turning your head 90 degrees. Are you ready?

Second exercise: give way by turning left.

Ready, set, go! Close your eyes and, while staying relaxed, mentally imagine adjusting your approach speed to have three options: go straight, slow down or stop. Also, add the left preselection using the right and left rearview mirrors and turning your head 90 degrees. Repeat this exercise 5 times with your eyes closed. Done? Now, still with your eyes closed, repeat the second exercise and add a move to the left, if the space is clear, to favor the flow of traffic, about 5 meters away from the give way point.

Third exercise: give way by turning left.

Ready, set, go! Close your eyes and, while staying relaxed, mentally imagine: Adjusting your approach speed to have three options: go, slow down, and eventually stop. Checking the right and left rearview mirrors. Turning your head 90 degrees to check for any vehicles in the left lane. Moving to the left, if space is available, to promote traffic flow, at about 5 meters from the give-way point. Adding deceleration to find the arrival point. Repeat this exercise five times with your eyes closed. Have you done it?
Fourth Exercise: Give way by turning left

Ready, set, go! Close your eyes and, while staying relaxed, mentally imagine:
Adjusting your approach speed to have the three possibilities: go, slow down, and stop. Then, check the right and left rearview mirrors, turn your head 90 degrees to look to your left and find the arrival point. Move to the left to promote traffic flow, at about 5 meters from the give-way point, and then slow down to find the arrival point. Repeat this exercise five times with your eyes closed. Have you done it? Now, still with your eyes closed, repeat the fifth exercise and imagine making a left lane change, checking blind spots and signaling your intention correctly.

Fifth exercise: giving way by turning left

Ready, set, go: Close your eyes and, while remaining relaxed, mentally imagine: Adjusting your approach speed to give you the 3 options: go, slow down, and stop; checking the right and left rearview mirrors; turning your head 90 degrees; moving to the left to promote traffic flow, about 5 meters from giving way; slowing down to find the destination point; looking for the destination point on your left; with a quick glance (0.25 seconds), checking the space on your left and right. Repeat this exercise 5 times with your eyes closed. Did you do it?

Sixth exercise: giving way by turning left

Ready, set, go: Close your eyes and, while remaining relaxed, mentally imagine:
Adjusting your approach speed to give you the 3 options: go, slow down, and stop; checking the right and left rearview mirrors; turning your head 90 degrees; moving to the left to promote traffic flow, about 5 meters from giving way; slowing down to find the destination point; looking for the destination point on your left; with a quick glance (0.25 seconds), checking the space on your left and right. If the space is free for about 5 meters, reach the destination point on your left by turning the steering wheel at the height of the mirror halfway to the road you need to reach. In this way, you will avoid invading the opposite lane. Repeat this exercise 5 times with your eyes closed. Did you do it?

Seventh exercise - Giving priority by turning left

Ready, set, go: Close your eyes and, while remaining relaxed, mentally imagine:
Adjust your approach speed so that you have three options: to go, slow down and stop.
Check the right rearview mirror and left rearview mirror.
Turn your head 90 degrees.
Move to the left to favor traffic flow.
About 5 meters before giving priority, slow down and look for the arrival point.
Look for the arrival point on your right.
With a glance (0.25 seconds), check the space on your left and right.
If the space is clear for about 5 meters, reach the arrival point on your left by turning the steering wheel at the height of the mirror halfway along the road you need to reach. You will avoid invading the opposite lane. Repeat this exercise 5 times always with your eyes closed. Have you done it?
14th exercise - Making giving priority by turning left automatic. Let's do it: Close your eyes and visualize the road where you perform the exercise. Mentally repeat this exercise 14 times. Are you ready? Ready, set, go: Adjust your approach speed. Check the right rearview mirror and left rearview mirror. Turn your head 90 degrees. Move to the left to favor traffic flow. Slow down. Look for the arrival point on your right. Check the space on your left and right. Reach the arrival point. Your brain has recorded everything in such a way that you no longer have to think about these 7 elements, while still keeping intact the 7 elements used by your consciousness. Try it on the road and you will see how giving priority by turning left will no longer be a problem for you.

Stop.

I have some questions for you:
Why was this signal created? Answer: First of all, for road safety, as with all signals related to road traffic.
What is its main characteristic? Answer: Its main characteristic is the obligation to come to a complete stop. In Switzerland, not coming to a complete stop at a stop sign is punishable with a fine of 60 Swiss francs.
Why do I have to come to a complete stop at a stop sign? Answer: The stop sign is always placed where visibility is insufficient to make the movement of vehicles safe at an intersection, junction, or fork where there is a case of priority. In other words, where two vehicles that are proceeding meet.

If you remember what was described at the beginning of this book, or rather, that our conscious mind can only handle 7 elements consciously, you immediately understand how important the behaviors (automatisms) that we apply when driving a vehicle are. Unlike giving priority where we look for the arrival point forward or sideways about 5 meters on the road to be traveled, at the stop sign, we have the arrival point that corresponds to the white line or, in its absence, to the end of the road that I am traveling on.

Let's start with the technique of learning through visualization for straight stops.

First exercise: straight stop with free space.

Ready, set, go: Close your eyes and, while remaining relaxed, imagine adjusting your approach speed so that you can stop at the white line or at the end of the road. Repeat this exercise 5 times with your eyes closed. Did you do it?

Second exercise: straight stop with free space and finding the stopping point.

Ready, set, go: Close your eyes and, while remaining relaxed, imagine adjusting your approach speed so that you can stop at the white line or at the end of the road, and finding the stopping point. Repeat this exercise 5 times with your eyes closed. Did you do it?

Third exercise: straight stop with free space,

finding the stopping point, and identifying free space on the left and right with a glance of 0.25 seconds. Ready, set, go: Close your eyes and, while remaining relaxed, imagine adjusting your approach speed so that you can stop at the white line or at the end of the road, finding the stopping point, and identifying free space on the left and right with a glance of 0.25 seconds. Repeat this exercise 5 times with your eyes closed. Did you do it?

Fourth exercise: straight stop with free space, finding the stopping point, identifying free space on the left and right with a glance of 0.25 seconds, and arriving at the previously sought stopping point. Ready, set, go: Close your eyes and, while remaining relaxed, imagine adjusting your approach speed so that you can stop at the white line or at the end of the road, finding the stopping point, identifying free space on the left and right with a glance of 0.25 seconds, and arriving at the previously sought stopping point. Repeat this exercise 5 times with your eyes closed. Did you do it?

Make the straight stop exercise automatic.

Let's do it:
Close your eyes, visualize the road where you are doing the exercise, and repeat it 14 times. Are you ready? Ready, set, go: Adjust your approach speed. Find the stopping point. Look for free space on your left and right. Go to the previously sought stopping point. Your brain has recorded everything so that you no longer have to consciously think about these 4 elements while maintaining the 7 elements used by your conscious mind. Try driving on the road and see how the straight stop with occupied spaces will no longer be a problem for you.

First exercise: straight stop with occupied space.

Ready, set, go: Close your eyes and, while remaining relaxed, imagine adjusting your approach speed so that you can stop at the white line or at the end of the road, even with occupied spaces. Repeat this exercise 5 times with your eyes closed. Did you do it? Now, still with your eyes closed, repeat the first exercise and add finding the stopping point.

Second exercise: straight stop with occupied space.

Ready, set, go: Close your eyes and, while staying relaxed, imagine yourself adjusting your approach speed so that you can stop at the white line or end of the road, searching for your destination point. Repeat this exercise 5 times with your eyes closed. Did you do it? Now, still with your eyes closed, repeat the second exercise and add the search for free space on your left and right with a glance of 0.25 seconds.

Third Exercise straight stop with occupied space.

Ready, set, go: Close your eyes and, while staying relaxed, mentally imagine:
Adjust your approach speed so that you can stop at the white line or end of the road, search for your destination point, look for free space on your left and right with a glance of 0.25 seconds. Repeat this exercise 5 times with your eyes closed. Did you do it?
Now, still with your eyes closed, repeat the third exercise and add: if the space is occupied, search for the destination point again.

Fourth Exercise straight stop with occupied space.

Ready, set, go: Close your eyes and, while staying relaxed, mentally imagine:
Adjust your approach speed so that you can stop at the white line or end of the road, search for your destination point, look for free space on your left and right with a glance of 0.25 seconds, if the space is occupied search for the destination point again. Repeat this exercise 5 times with your eyes closed. Did you do it? Now, still with your eyes closed, repeat the fourth exercise and add: if the space is still occupied, search for free space on your left and right with a glance of 0.25 seconds again.

Fifth Exercise straight stop with occupied space.

Ready, set, go:
Close your eyes and, while staying relaxed, mentally imagine:
Adjust your approach speed so that you can stop at the white line or end of the road, search for your destination point, look for free space on your left and right with a glance of 0.25 seconds, if the space is occupied search for the destination point again, if the space is still occupied search for free space on your left and right with a glance of 0.25 seconds again. If the space is free, go to the destination point. If, instead, the space is still occupied, repeat the iteration by searching for the destination point and free space again until it becomes available. Repeat this exercise 5 times with your eyes closed. Did you do it?
Ready, set, go:
Close your eyes and, while relaxed, mentally imagine:
Adjusting the approach speed to be able to stop at the white line or end of the road.

Performing the preselection to the right.
Searching for the destination point.
Looking for free space on your left and right.
Searching for the destination point again, if necessary.
Checking for the presence of other vehicles or obstacles near the intersection, by looking in the rearview mirrors and turning your head 90 degrees to the right to check for any vehicles on the right lane. Stop at the white line or end of the road, and if the space is clear, proceed to the right.
Repeat this exercise 5 times with your eyes closed. Have you done it?
This exercise will help you memorize the necessary steps to perform a right stop with preselection and develop the ability to check the mirrors and turn your head to check for any vehicles before proceeding to the right.

Second exercise: right stop with preselection.
Ready, set, go:

First exercise right stop with preselection.

: Close your eyes and, in a relaxed state, mentally imagine adjusting your approach speed so that you can stop at the white line or end of the road. Then imagine looking at the left mirror, then the right mirror, and finally turning your head 90 degrees to the right. Repeat this exercise 5 times with your eyes closed. Second exercise: Still with your eyes closed, repeat the first exercise and add the gesture of indicating right. Third exercise: Imagine adjusting your approach speed so that you can stop at the white line or end of the road, look at the left mirror, then the right mirror and turn your head 90 degrees to the right. Then, still with your eyes closed, imagine indicating right and making a right turn about 5 meters before the stop line. Repeat this exercise 5 times. Fourth exercise: still with your eyes closed, repeat the third exercise and add the action of stopping at the white line after moving to the right. Repeat this exercise 5 times.

Fifth exercise: right turn with lane pre-selection.

Ready, set, go: Close your eyes and, while relaxed, imagine: Adjusting your approach speed to be able to stop at the white line or end of the road. Checking (left mirror, right mirror, turn your head 90 degrees to the right). Indicating a right turn. Moving to the right about 5 meters before the stop line. Stopping at the white line.

Repeat this exercise 5 times always with your eyes closed. Have you done it? Now, still with your eyes closed, repeat the sixth exercise and add: Finding the point of arrival on your right. Looking for space on the left of about 5 meters. If it's clear, proceed to the point of arrival on the right. Repeat this exercise 5 times always with your eyes closed. Have you done it? Close your eyes and visualize the road where you are doing the exercise and repeat it 14 times. Are you ready? On your mark: Adjust the approach speed to be able to stop at the white line. Look. Signal right. Move to the right. Look for the arrival point on your right. Look for space on the left. If it's free, proceed to the arrival point on the right. Go to the arrival point. Your brain has recorded everything so that you no longer have to think about these 7 elements while keeping intact the 7 elements used by your conscious mind. Try it on the road and you'll see how the right turn with preselection will no longer be a problem for you.

First exercise - left turn with preselection:

On your mark: Close your eyes and, while relaxed, imagine adjusting the approach speed so that you can stop at the white line or at the end of the road. Repeat this exercise 5 times with your eyes closed. Done? Now, still with your eyes closed, repeat the first exercise and add "look" (check the right mirror, left mirror, and turn your head 90 degrees to the right).

Second exercise - left turn with preselection:

On your mark: Close your eyes and, while relaxed, imagine adjusting the approach speed so that you can stop at the white line or at the end of the road. Add "look" (check the right mirror, left mirror, and turn your head 90 degrees to the left) and repeat the exercise 5 times with your eyes closed. Done? Now, still with your eyes closed, repeat the second exercise and add "signal left".

Third exercise - left turn with preselection:

On your mark: Close your eyes and, while relaxed, mentally imagine adjusting the approach speed so that you can stop at the white line or at the end of the road. Then add the following steps: Look: right mirror, left mirror, turn your head 90 degrees to the left. Signal left. Move to the left (about 5 meters before the stop line). Stop at the white line. Repeat this exercise 5 times with your eyes closed. Done? Now, still with your eyes closed, repeat the fifth exercise and add the right turn (about 5 meters before the stop line) after putting on the left turn signal and making the left turn. Repeat this exercise 5 times with your eyes closed. Did you do it? Now, still with your eyes closed, repeat the sixth exercise and add looking for space on the right and oncoming traffic (about 5 meters). If clear, make the right turn and go to the destination point on the left using the mirror technique.

Seventh Exercise - Left turn with preselection:

Ready, set, go: Close your eyes and, while relaxed, mentally imagine adjusting your approach speed so that you can stop at the white line or at the end of the road. Look (right mirror, left mirror, turn head 90 degrees to the left), put on the right turn signal, make the left turn (about 5 meters before the stop line), stop at the white line, look for the destination point on your left, look for space on the right and oncoming traffic (about 5 meters). If clear, make the right turn and go to the destination point on the left using the mirror technique. Repeat this exercise 5 times with your eyes closed. Did you do it?

Exercise 18: Make the Stop exercise automatic,

making the right turn with preselection.

Let's do it:

Close your eyes, visualize the road where you are doing the exercise, and repeat it 14 times. Are you ready?

Ready, set, go: Adjust the speed of approach. Look. Signal left. Move to the left lane. Look for the destination on your left. Check for space on the right and oncoming traffic. Go to the destination. Your brain has recorded everything so that you don't have to consciously think about these 7 elements, while still retaining the 7 elements used by your consciousness. Try it on the road and see how left turns with preselection will no longer be a problem for you. Changing lanes on straight roads. Let's begin with the visualization learning technique for lanes.

First exercise: Traveling on the right lane in the city.

Ready, set, go:Close your eyes and, while being relaxed, mentally imagine:

Adjusting the speed on the right lane according to speed limits and traffic flow. Repeat this exercise 5 times with your eyes closed.

Now, still with your eyes closed, repeat the first exercise and add the trajectory corresponding to the left wheel of the four-wheeled vehicle in front of you.

Second exercise: Traveling on the right lane in the city.

Ready, set, go:

Close your eyes and, while being relaxed, mentally imagine:

Adjusting the speed on the right lane according to speed limits and traffic flow.

Adding the trajectory corresponding to the left wheel of the four-wheeled vehicle in front of you. Repeat this exercise 5 times with your eyes closed.

Let's begin with the visualization learning technique for lanes.

First exercise: Traveling on the right lane in the city.

Ready, set, go:
Close your eyes and, while being relaxed, mentally imagine yourself on the right lane. Adjust your speed according to speed limits and traffic flow. Repeat this exercise 5 times, always with your eyes closed.
Now, still with your eyes closed, repeat the first exercise and add the trajectory corresponding to the left wheel of the four-wheeled vehicle in front of you.
Second exercise: Making the exercise of the right lane with the trajectory corresponding to the left wheel of the four-wheeled vehicle in front of you automatic.
Let's do it:
Close your eyes and visualize the road where you are doing the exercise. Repeat the exercise 14 times. Are you ready?
Ready, set, go:
Regulate your speed.
Add the trajectory corresponding to the left wheel of the four-wheeled vehicle in front of you.
Your brain has registered everything so that you no longer have to think about these two elements, while keeping the 7 elements used by your conscious mind intact. Try going on the road and you will see how the right lane with space on the right will no longer be a problem for you.
Now, still with your eyes closed, repeat the first exercise on the left lane.

First exercise: driving on the left lane in the city.
Ready, set, go:
On the left lane, regulate your speed according to the speed limit and traffic flow. Repeat this exercise 5 times always with your eyes closed.
Now, still with your eyes closed, repeat the first exercise and add the trajectory corresponding to the left wheel of the four-wheeled vehicle that precedes you.
Second exercise: make the exercise of the left lane with the trajectory corresponding to the left wheel of the four-wheeled vehicle that precedes you automatic.

Ready, set, go:

Close your eyes and, while relaxed, mentally visualize yourself on the left lane. Adjust your speed according to the speed limit and traffic flow, adding the trajectory corresponding to the left wheel of the four-wheeled vehicle in front of you. Repeat this exercise 5 times, always with your eyes closed. Have you done it?

Automate the lane change from right to left in the city with the trajectory corresponding to the left wheel of the four-wheeled vehicle in front of you.
Let's do it:
Close your eyes, visualize the road where you'll be doing the exercise, and repeat this exercise 14 times. Are you ready?

Ready, set, go:
Adjust your speed.
Add the trajectory corresponding to the left wheel of the four-wheel vehicle ahead of you.
Your brain has recorded everything so that you no longer have to think about these 2 elements, while keeping the 7 elements used by your consciousness intact. Try going on the road and you will see how the lane change from right to left, with space on the right, will no longer be a problem for you.
First Exercise: Lane change from right to left in the city.
Ready, set, go:
Close your eyes and, while relaxed, mentally imagine:
Adjust your speed on the right lane according to the speed limit and traffic flow. Repeat this exercise 5 times always with your eyes closed. Have you done it?
Now, always with your eyes closed, repeat the first exercise and add the trajectory corresponding to the left wheel of the four-wheel vehicle ahead of you.
Second Exercise: Making the lane change from right to left in the city automatic with the trajectory corresponding to the left wheel of the four-wheel vehicle ahead of you.
Let's do it:
Close your eyes and, while relaxed, mentally imagine: Adjusting your speed on the right lane based on the speed limit and traffic flow. Following the trajectory of the left wheel of the four-wheel vehicle in front of you. Repeat this exercise 5 times with your eyes closed. Have you done it?

Fifth Exercise: Changing lanes from right to left in the city.
Ready, set, go:
Close your eyes and, while relaxed, imagine being on the right lane of an urban street. Adjust your speed based on the speed limit and traffic flow, while following the trajectory of the left wheel of the four-wheel vehicle in front of you. Keep moving and, using the left side mirror, look for an empty space on your left, paying attention to any vehicles or obstacles present. Turn your head 90 degrees to the left to better check for any obstacles and vehicles in the left lane.

Repeat this exercise mentally 5 times, always with your eyes closed, maintaining maximum attention and always checking for any vehicles or obstacles before making a lane change, ensuring maximum safety on the road.

Remember that safe driving requires maximum attention and caution in every situation, and that it is important to respect traffic laws and local regulations.

Ready, set, go: Close your eyes and, while staying relaxed, mentally imagine being on the right lane in the city. Adjust your speed according to the speed limits and traffic flow, keeping the trajectory corresponding to the left wheel of the four-wheel vehicle in front of you. Look forward to the left and find the dynamic endpoint on the left side through the left side mirror and look for an empty space on your left. Turn your head to the left by 90 degrees to check the free space on the left side. Repeat this exercise 5 times with your eyes closed. Did you do it? Now, still with your eyes closed, repeat the fifth exercise and add: if the space on your left side is clear, turn on the left turn signal.

Sixth exercise: lane change from the right to the left in the city. Ready, set, go: Close your eyes and, while staying relaxed, mentally imagine being on the right lane in the city. Adjust your speed according to the speed limits and traffic flow, keeping the trajectory corresponding to the left wheel of the four-wheel vehicle in front of you. Look forward to the left and find the dynamic endpoint on the left side through the left side mirror and look for an empty space on your left. Turn your head to the left by 90 degrees to check the free space on the left side. If the space on your left side is clear, turn on the left turn signal. Repeat this exercise 5 times with your eyes closed. Did you do it? Now, still with your eyes closed, repeat the sixth exercise and add: go to the previously searched endpoint. Remember to always use the utmost attention and to always check for the presence of any vehicles or obstacles before making a lane change in order to ensure maximum safety on the road.

Seventh exercise: changing lanes from the right to the left in the city.

Ready, set, go: Close your eyes and, while remaining relaxed, mentally imagine being on the right lane in the city. Adjust your speed according to the speed limit and traffic flow, maintaining the trajectory corresponding to the left wheel of the four-wheeled vehicle in front of you. Look forward to the left dynamic arrival point through the left side mirror and check for free space on your left. Turn your head 90 degrees to the left to check the free space on the left side. If the space on your left side is free, use the left turn signal and go to the previously selected arrival point. Repeat this exercise 5 times with your eyes closed. Have you done it? Now, make this exercise automatic.

Let's do it: Close your eyes, visualize the road where you will perform the exercise, and repeat it 14 times. Are you ready?

Here we go:

Adjust the speed.
Follow the trajectory corresponding to the right wheel of the four-wheel vehicle in front of you.
Look forward to the right for the dynamic endpoint.
Check the free space on your right using the right side mirror.
Turn your head to the right by 90 degrees.
Put the right turn signal on.
Reach the dynamic endpoint.

Your brain has recorded everything in such a way that you no longer have to consciously think about these 7 elements, while still keeping them intact. Try it on the road, and you'll see how changing lanes to the right will no longer be a problem for yo

First exercise for changing lanes from left to right in the city.

Ready, set, go: Close your eyes and, in a relaxed state, imagine:

On the right lane, adjust your speed according to the speed limits and traffic flow. Repeat this exercise 5 times with your eyes closed. Have you done it? Now, still with your eyes closed, repeat the first exercise and add the trajectory corresponding to the left wheel of the four-wheeled vehicle in front of you.

Second exercise for changing lanes from left to right in the city.

Ready, set, go: Close your eyes and, in a relaxed state, imagine:
On the right lane, adjust your speed according to the speed limits and traffic flow, and follow the trajectory corresponding to the left wheel of the four-wheeled vehicle in front of you. Repeat this exercise 5 times with your eyes closed.
Now, still with your eyes closed, repeat the second exercise and search forward on the right for the dynamic arrival point, where you intend to position the vehicle after changing lanes. Repeat this exercise 5 times. Have you done it?

Third Exercise: Changing Lanes from Left to Right in the City.

Ready, set, go: Close your eyes and, in a relaxed state, mentally imagine: On the right lane, adjust your speed based on the speed limits and traffic flow, follow the trajectory corresponding to the left wheel of the four-wheel vehicle in front of you, and search forward on the right for the dynamic end point. Repeat this exercise five times with your eyes closed. Have you done it? Now, still with your eyes closed, repeat the third exercise and, through the right side mirror, search for the free space on your right.

Fourth Exercise: Changing Lanes from Left to Right in the City.

Ready, set, go:Close your eyes and, in a relaxed state, mentally imagine: On the right lane, adjust your speed based on the speed limits and traffic flow, follow the trajectory corresponding to the left wheel of the four-wheel vehicle in front of you, search forward on the right for the dynamic end point, and verify through the right side mirror the free space on your right. Repeat this exercise five times with your eyes closed.

Now, still with your eyes closed, repeat the fourth exercise and turn your head 90 degrees to the right to check the free space on the left side of the road before changing lanes. Repeat this exercise five times. Have you done it?

Fifth Exercise lane change from the left to the right in the city.

Here we go:

Close your eyes and, while remaining relaxed, imagine yourself on the left lane and having to change to the right lane. Adjust your speed according to the speed limit and the flow of traffic, while maintaining the trajectory corresponding to the left wheel of the four-wheeled vehicle in front of you. Use the right side mirror to look for free space on your right. If the space on your right side is free, turn on the right indicator. Repeat this exercise 5 times with your eyes closed. Have you done it?
Now, with your eyes still closed, repeat the fifth exercise and add: if the space on your right side is free, turn on the right indicator.

Sixth Exercise lane change from the left to the right in the city.

Here we go:

Close your eyes and, while remaining relaxed, imagine yourself on the left lane and having to change to the right lane. Adjust your speed according to the speed limit and the flow of traffic, while maintaining the trajectory corresponding to the left wheel of the four-wheeled vehicle in front of you. Use the right side mirror to look for free space on your right. If the space on your right side is free, turn on the right indicator and proceed towards the previously searched arrival point. Repeat this exercise 5 times with your eyes closed. Have you done it?

Seventh Exercise: Changing lanes from the right to the left in the city.

Ready, set, go: Close your eyes and, feeling relaxed, imagine yourself in the right lane and needing to change to the left lane. Adjust your speed according to the speed limits and traffic flow, keeping the trajectory corresponding to the right wheel of the four-wheeled vehicle in front of you. Use the left side mirror to check for free space on your left. If the space on your left side is clear, turn on your left signal and proceed towards the desired endpoint. Repeat this exercise 5 times with your eyes closed. Have you done it?

Now let's make the exercise automatic:

Close your eyes, visualize the road where you will perform the exercise, and repeat it 14 times. Are you ready?

Ready, set, go:

Adjust speed
Keep the trajectory corresponding to the right wheel of the four-wheeled vehicle in front of you.
Look ahead to the left for the dynamic endpoint.
Check for free space on your left using the left side mirror.
Turn your head to the left at a 90-degree angle.
Turn on the left signal.
Reach the dynamic endpoint.
Your brain has recorded everything so that you don't have to think about these 7 steps anymore, while keeping intact the 7 elements used by your conscious mind. Try it on the road and you'll see how changing lanes to the left won't be a problem for you anymore.

Changing Lanes in a Roundabout.

It's done exactly like on a straight road. Let's make a lane change from the left lane to the right lane. Important: The right lane always has priority over the left lane.

First Exercise lane change from left to right in a roundabout.

Let's go: Close your eyes and, while relaxed, mentally imagine yourself on the right lane. Adjust your speed according to the speed limit and traffic flow. Repeat this exercise 5 times with your eyes closed. Have you done it?

Now, still with your eyes closed, repeat the first exercise and add the trajectory corresponding to the left wheel of the four-wheeled vehicle in front of you.

Second Exercise: Lane change from left to right in a roundabout.

Ready, set, go: Close your eyes and, while staying relaxed, mentally imagine: On the right lane, adjust your speed based on the speed limits and traffic flow, while following the trajectory corresponding to the left wheel of the four-wheeled vehicle in front of you. Repeat this exercise five times with your eyes closed. Have you done it? Now, still with your eyes closed, repeat the second exercise and add the search for the dynamic arrival point on the right side.

Third Exercise: Lane change from left to right in a roundabout.

Ready, set, go: Close your eyes and, while staying relaxed, mentally imagine: On the right lane, adjust your speed based on the speed limits and traffic flow, while following the trajectory corresponding to the left wheel of the four-wheeled vehicle in front of you, and search for the dynamic arrival point on the right side. Repeat this exercise five times with your eyes closed. Have you done it? Now, still with your eyes closed, repeat the third exercise and, using the right-side mirror, search for the free space on your right.

Fourth Exercise: Lane change from left to right in a roundabout.

Ready, set, go: Close your eyes and, while staying relaxed, mentally imagine:
On the right lane, adjust your speed based on the speed limits and traffic flow, while following the trajectory corresponding to the left wheel of the four-wheeled vehicle in front of you, search for the dynamic arrival point on the right side, and using the right-side mirror, search for the free space on your right. Repeat this exercise five times with your eyes closed. Have you done it?

Now, still with your eyes closed, repeat the fourth exercise and add the instruction to turn your head 90 degrees to the left to check for free space on the left side.

The Fifth Exercise involves changing lanes from the left to the right in a roundabout. Ready, set, go: Close your eyes and, in a relaxed state, mentally imagine: Adjusting your speed on the right lane according to the speed limit and traffic flow. Maintaining the trajectory corresponding to the left wheel of the four-wheeled vehicle in front of you. Searching ahead on the right for the dynamic arrival point, using the right side mirror. Checking for free space on your right side. Turning your head 90 degrees to the left to check for free space on the left side. If the space on your right side is clear, signal and change lanes to the right. Repeat this exercise 5 times with your eyes closed. Have you completed the Fifth Exercise?

The Sixth Exercise involves changing lanes from the left to the right in a roundabout. Ready, set, go: Close your eyes and, in a relaxed state, mentally imagine performing the same steps as in the Fifth Exercise, but this time on the left lane of the roundabout. If the space on your right side is clear, signal and change lanes to the right. Repeat this exercise 5 times with your eyes closed. Have you completed the Sixth Exercise?

Ready, set, go: Close your eyes and, in a relaxed state, imagine yourself on the right lane of a roundabout. Adjust your speed according to the speed limit and traffic flow, trying to follow the trajectory corresponding to the left wheel of the four-wheeled vehicle in front of you. Search ahead on the right for the dynamic arrival point using the right side mirror, check for free space on your right side, and turn your head 90 degrees to the right to check for free space on the left side. If the space on your right side is clear, signal and proceed to the previously searched dynamic arrival point. Repeat this exercise 5 times with your eyes closed. Have you completed it?

To automate the lane change exercise from the left to the right in a roundabout, close your eyes and visualize the road where you will perform the exercise. Repeat the exercise 14 times. Are you ready?

Ready, set, go:
Adjust your speed.
Follow the trajectory corresponding to the left wheel of the four-wheeled vehicle in front of you.
Search ahead on the right for the dynamic arrival point.
Use the right side mirror to check for free space on your right side.
Turn your head 90 degrees to the right.
Signal right if the space on your right side is clear.
Proceed to the dynamic arrival point.
Your brain has registered all of this so that you don't have to consciously think about these 7 elements, keeping them intact in your consciousness. Try it on the road and you'll see how changing lanes to the right in a roundabout will no longer be a problem for you. Highway, expressway, speed, entrance, exit, speed limits.

Can everyone go on the highway?

Answer:

Each country in Europe has more or less the same rules, which can vary for learner drivers and for the categories of license allowed in the A category. In Switzerland, all vehicles belonging to categories A, B, and higher are allowed. For category A1, vehicles with at least 125cc are allowed. All drivers who have a driving license, including learner drivers, are authorized when their driving preparation allows it and before taking the practical exam.

At what speed can you go? Answer: In Europe, the speed limits of each country are indicated at the entrance of the country. In Switzerland, the speed limit is 120 km/h, in Italy and France it is 130 km/h, and in Germany, for now, there are no speed limits imposed, although the routes where this lack of limit applies are few. It is important to know that at the entrance and exit of the highway, the speed is regulated in such a way that those entering the highway can better use the necessary space.

Do you have to pay tolls on the highway? Answer: In almost all European countries, except for Germany for now, you have to pay for its use. In Switzerland, there is a fixed tax, which in 2021 is CHF 40 and is valid for the entire year in which it is paid, not for a year (12 months), but for the current year. In other countries, tolls are paid at the toll booths. The use of a telepass, which allows you to pay the toll directly from your bank account or through the service company, is very common.

What is the purpose of the acceleration lane?

Answer: It is used to reach the correct speed that makes it possible to enter the right lane of the highway. In case of need, it is possible to continue on the emergency lane to enter the highway.

What is the purpose of the deceleration lane? Answer: It is used to slow down while exiting the highway. The exit must be made at the same speed so that the vehicle that continues on the highway does not have to slow down because of you (traffic flow).

When should you signal your exit on the highway? Answer: About 300 meters before the exit.

Can you overtake before an exit on the highway? Answer: Overtaking is prohibited from 1000 meters before the exit.

When should you start an overtaking maneuver on the highway? Answer: In general, you start the overtaking maneuver when you have enough space, usually just before reaching the safety distance (2 seconds).

When should you return to the right lane after overtaking? Answer: You should return from overtaking when you see the vehicle you passed in your center rearview mirror.

What is the purpose of the emergency lane? Answer: The emergency lane is used to allow vehicles in trouble or involved in an accident to safely stop outside the highway lane. In addition, the emergency lane is also used to allow access to law enforcement or emergency responders in case of an emergency. It is important to remember that the emergency lane should not be used as a passing lane.

Let's start with the technique of learning through visualization
for entering the highway from the acceleration lane.

First exercise:

Are you ready? Close your eyes and relax. Now, mentally imagine yourself on the acceleration lane and adjust your speed according to the speed limits and traffic flow, keeping it between 80 and 90 km/h depending on the imposed limits. Repeat this exercise 5 times with your eyes closed. Done?

Now, still with your eyes closed, repeat the second exercise and add, if the space is clear, turning your head 90 degrees to check for any vehicles on the right lane (a glance of about 0.25 seconds). Repeat this exercise 5 times with your eyes closed. Have you done it?

Third exercise, entering the highway from the acceleration lane. Ready, set, go:

Close your eyes and, while relaxed, mentally imagine yourself: On the acceleration lane Adjusting your speed based on the speed limits and traffic flow between 80 and 90 km/h depending on the imposed limits, searching for space on the right lane of the highway using the left side mirror, and if the space is clear, turning your head 90 degrees (a glance of 0.25 seconds). Repeat this exercise 5 times with your eyes closed. Have you done it?

Now, still with your eyes closed, repeat the third exercise and add, if the space is clear, turning on the left turn signal.
Fourth exercise, entering the highway from the acceleration lane.

Ready, set, go: Close your eyes and, feeling relaxed, mentally imagine: On the acceleration lane, adjust your speed based on the speed limits and traffic flow, keeping it between 80 and 90 km/h depending on the limits set. Use your left-side mirror to search for space on the right-hand lane of the highway. If space is available, turn your head 90 degrees to check (0.25-second glance) and, if there's space, signal to the left. Repeat this exercise five times with your eyes closed. Have you done it?

Now, still with your eyes closed, repeat the fourth exercise, adding the search for the dynamic point of arrival on the right-hand lane of the highway, about 25-30 meters ahead of you.

Fifth Exercise: Entry onto the highway from the acceleration lane.

Ready, set, go: Close your eyes and, feeling relaxed, mentally imagine: On the acceleration lane, adjust your speed based on the speed limits and traffic flow, keeping it between 80 and 90 km/h depending on the limits set. Use your left-side mirror to search for space on the right-hand lane of the highway. If space is available, turn your head 90 degrees to check (0.25-second glance), signal to the left if there's space, and search for the dynamic point of arrival on the right-hand lane of the highway, about 25-30 meters ahead of you. Repeat this exercise five times with your eyes closed. Have you done it? Now, still with your eyes closed, repeat the fifth exercise and add giving full throttle to reach the dynamic arrival point.

Sixth Exercise: Entering the highway from the acceleration lane.

Ready, set, go: Close your eyes and, while remaining relaxed, mentally imagine: Adjusting the speed on the acceleration lane according to the speed limits and traffic flow, maintaining it between 80 and 90 km/h depending on the imposed limits. Searching for space on the right lane of the highway using the left side mirror. If space is available, turn your head 90 degrees (in a 0.25-second glance) and, if the space is free, signal left. Searching for the dynamic arrival point on the right lane of the highway about 25-30 meters away. Giving full throttle to reach the arrival point. Repeat this exercise 5 times always with your eyes closed. Have you done it?

Exercise 24: Automatic highway entry.

Let's do it: Close your eyes and visualize the road where you're doing the exercise. Repeat it 14 times. Are you ready?

Ready, set, go: Adjust the speed according to the speed limits and traffic flow, keeping it between 80 and 90 km/h depending on the imposed limits.
Search for space on the right lane of the highway using the left side mirror.

Turn your head 90 degrees to check if the space on the right lane is free (in a glance of about 0.25 seconds). If space is available, signal left. Search for the dynamic arrival point on the right lane of the highway about 25-30 meters ahead of you. Give full throttle to reach the arrival point.

Your brain has recorded everything so that you no longer have to think about these 6 elements, while keeping intact the 7 elements used by your consciousness. Try going on the highway and you'll see how the entry won't be a problem for you anymore.

Highway exit

First Exercise for exiting the highway: Ready, set, go: Close your eyes and, while remaining relaxed, mentally imagine: On the highway, approximately 500 meters before your exit, adjust your speed to around 90 km/h, but not below 80 km/h if traffic and speed limits allow. Repeat this exercise 5 times with your eyes closed. Have you done it? Now, still with your eyes closed, repeat the first exercise and at 300 meters, turn on your right turn signal.

Second Exercise for exiting the highway:

Ready, set, go: Close your eyes and, while remaining relaxed, mentally imagine: On the highway, approximately 500 meters before your exit, adjust your speed to around 90 km/h, but not below 80 km/h if traffic and speed limits allow. At 300 meters, turn on your right turn signal. Repeat this exercise 5 times with your eyes closed. Have you done it? Now, still with your eyes closed, repeat the second exercise and follow the white line on the right side.

Third Exercise for exiting the highway:

Ready, set, go: Close your eyes and, while remaining relaxed, mentally imagine:
On the highway, approximately 500 meters before your exit, adjust your speed to around 90 km/h, but not below 80 km/h if traffic and speed limits allow. At 300 meters, turn on your right turn signal and follow the white line on the right side. Repeat this exercise 5 times with your eyes closed. Have you done it? Exiting the highway must be done on the right lane and you must check that your speed is in line with the imposed limits and traffic conditions. Moreover, before doing the exercise on the road, make sure you have a good understanding of road signs and safety regulations to avoid accidents. Now, still with your eyes closed, repeat the third exercise and add searching for the exit point on the deceleration lane.

Fourth Highway Exit Exercise:

Ready, set, go: Close your eyes and, while relaxing, mentally imagine: On the highway, about 500 meters before the exit, adjust your speed to around 90 km/h, not below 80 km/h, depending on traffic and speed limits. At 300 meters, turn on your right turn signal, follow the white line on your right, and search for the exit point on the deceleration lane. Repeat this exercise 5 times with your eyes closed. Have you done it? Now, still with your eyes closed, repeat the fourth exercise and add searching for the dynamic exit point on the deceleration lane, following the white line on your right and maintaining the same speed.

Fifth Highway Exit Exercise:

Ready, set, go: Close your eyes and, while relaxing, mentally imagine:

On the highway, about 500 meters before the exit, adjust your speed to around 90 km/h, not below 80 km/h, depending on traffic and speed limits. At 300 meters, turn on your right turn signal, follow the white line on your right, search for the dynamic exit point on the deceleration lane, and go to the dynamic exit point while maintaining the same speed, following the white line on your right. Repeat this exercise 5 times with your eyes closed. Have you done it?

Now, always with your eyes closed, repeat the fourth exercise and add: when you reach the dynamic braking lane, brake the vehicle to adjust the speed (usually 60 km/h).

Sixth exercise: highway exit.

Ready, set, go: Close your eyes and, while feeling relaxed, imagine yourself on the highway about 500 meters before the exit. Adjust your speed to about 90 km/h, not going below 80 km/h if traffic and speed limits allow it. At 300 meters from the exit, turn on the right turn signal and follow the white line on the right side. Look for the dynamic arrival point on the deceleration lane, and following the white line on your right, go to the dynamic arrival point always at the same speed. When you reach the dynamic braking lane, brake the vehicle to adjust the speed (usually 60 km/h). Repeat this exercise 5 times always with your eyes closed. Have you done it?

25 - Making the highway exit exercise automatic.

Let's do it:

Close your eyes, visualize the road where you do the exercise, and repeat it 14 times. Are you ready?

Here we go:
Adjust the speed.
At 300 meters from the exit, turn on the right signal.
Follow the right white sideline.
Look for the dynamic arrival point on the deceleration lane.
Go to the dynamic arrival point.
Brake the vehicle to adjust the speed.
Your brain has recorded everything so that you don't have to think about these 6 elements anymore, while keeping the 7 elements used by your consciousness intact. Try to go on the highway, and you'll see how the exit won't be a problem for you anymore.

Safe distance:

To calculate the distance to keep from the vehicle in front, called the safe distance, the 2-second technique is used. This technique is practically always used. Here's how to apply it:
Find a fixed reference point on the road, such as a post, a sign or other.
Observe when the vehicle in front of you passes this reference point, count (21..22) and check at the end of the count where your vehicle is compared to the point previously chosen.
If you have passed the reference point, it means that you are too close to the vehicle in front of you. If you are on the reference point or just before, it means that you are respecting the safe distance.
If you are still far away, it means that you are still too early to overtake on the highway, in case of overtaking on the highway.

Semi Highway, speed, entrance, exit, speed limits:

In the Semi motorways have a maximum speed limit of 100 km/h, which is always indicated by road signs. There are not always acceleration and deceleration lanes like on motorways. Additionally, unlike motorways, there is only one lane and oncoming traffic. The technique used is similar to that

used on motorways, with the most important difference being that the space available is generally more limited. To calculate the distance to keep from the vehicle in front, known as the safe distance, the two-second rule is used. This technique is used practically always. Here's how to apply it:
Find a fixed reference point on the road, such as a post or a sign.
Observe when the vehicle in front passes this reference point.
Mentally count two seconds as the vehicle in front moves away from the reference point.
At the end of the count, check where your vehicle is in relation to the previously chosen point.
If you are on or just before the reference point, you are respecting the safe distance.
If you have already passed the reference point, you are too close to the vehicle in front and need to increase your distance.
If you are still far from the reference point, it means you are still too far from the safe distance and cannot overtake on the motorway.
As for overtaking on the motorway, it is recommended to start the overtaking manoeuvre at a safe distance (two seconds) to avoid exiting too early and causing problems for traffic already on the right lane. After overtaking, return to the right lane at a distance that does not put the overtaken vehicle in difficulty.

Regarding visualization exercises, here's how you could rephrase the text: Visualization exercise for overtaking on the highway: Close your eyes and relax. Imagine approaching the vehicle ahead of you in the right lane. Visualize the fixed reference point on the road. Observe when the vehicle ahead of you passes this reference point. Mentally count two seconds as the vehicle ahead of you moves away from the reference point. Imagine beginning the overtaking maneuver at the end of the count. Visualize your vehicle moving to the left lane to overtake the vehicle ahead of you. Imagine the vehicle you have passed moving away. Visualize the moment you return to the right lane after overtaking, at a distance that does not pose a problem for the passed vehicle. Repeat the exercise mentally several times, until you feel confident and know the procedure by heart.

Fifth Exercise: Overtaking on the highway exiting to the left lane.

Ready, set, go: Close your eyes and, while staying relaxed, imagine approaching the vehicle in front of you on the right lane. Look for a fixed reference point where the vehicle in front of you passes, establish a safe distance (count to 21-22 and check if your passage from the fixed point corresponds to the end of the count), stabilize your speed while keeping a safe distance, and look for the space on the left lane using the left side mirror. Repeat this exercise five times with your eyes closed. Have you done it? Now, still with your eyes closed, repeat the fifth exercise and add "Once you've found the free space, turn your head 90 degrees to the left to check the space on your left."

Sixth Exercise: Overtaking on the highway exiting to the left lane.

Ready, set, go: Close your eyes and, while staying relaxed, imagine approaching the vehicle in front of you on the right lane. Look for a fixed reference point where the vehicle in front of you passes, establish a safe distance (count to 21-22 and check if your passage from the fixed point corresponds to the end of the count), stabilize your speed while keeping a safe distance, look for the space on the left lane using the left side mirror, once you've found the free space, turn your head 90 degrees to the left to check the space on your left. After verifying the space on your left, look for the dynamic point on the left lane, put on your turn signal, and reach it. Repeat this exercise five times with your eyes closed. Have you done it?

Seventh Exercise: Overtaking on the highway, exiting on the left lane.

Get ready: Close your eyes and, while relaxed, mentally imagine: Approaching the vehicle ahead of you on the right lane. Looking for a fixed point where the vehicle passes. Establishing a safe distance by counting to 21-22 and verifying if the passing from the fixed point corresponds to the end of the count. Stabilizing the speed while keeping the safe distance. Checking for space on the left lane from the left side mirror. Turning your head 90 degrees to the left to check the space on your left. Checking the space on your left, finding the dynamic point on the left lane, signaling and reaching it.

Repeat this exercise 5 times with your eyes closed. Have you done it?

Automating the overtaking on the highway, exiting on the left lane exercise.
Let's do it:
Close your eyes and visualize the road where you're doing the exercise. Repeat this exercise 14 times to automate the process.
Get ready:
Approaching the vehicle ahead of you on the right lane.
Looking for a fixed point.
Establishing a safe distance and stabilizing the speed.
Checking for space on the left lane from the mirror.
Turning your head 90 degrees to the left to check the space on your left.
Checking the space on your left, finding the dynamic point on the left lane, signaling and reaching it.
Your brain has recorded everything in such a way that you no longer have to think about these 7 elements, while keeping intact the 7 elements used by your conscious mind.

First exercise, overtaking on the highway and returning to the right lane.

Ready, set, go: Close your eyes and, while relaxed, imagine:
Maintaining a constant speed
Overtaking a vehicle on the left lane
Returning to the right lane while maintaining a safe distance from the passed vehicle
Repeat this exercise 5 times with your eyes closed. Did you do it?
Now, still with your eyes closed, repeat the first exercise and add:
Checking for the passed vehicle in the rearview mirror
Second exercise, overtaking on the highway and returning to the right lane.
Ready, set, go: Close your eyes and, while relaxed, imagine:
Maintaining a constant speed

Overtaking a vehicle on the left lane

Checking for the passed vehicle in the rearview mirror
Using the right turn signal to indicate returning to the right lane
Repeat this exercise 5 times with your eyes closed. Did you do it?

Third Exercise highway overtaking returning to the right lane. Ready, set, go: Close your eyes and, while relaxed, imagine: Maintaining a constant speed Overtaking a vehicle on the left lane Checking the overtaken vehicle in the rear-view mirror Putting on the right turn signal to signal the return to the right lane Returning to the right lane while maintaining a safe distance from the overtaken vehicle Repeat this exercise 5 times with your eyes closed. Have you done it?

First Exercise highway overtaking return to the right lane.

Ready, set, go: Close your eyes and, while remaining relaxed, mentally imagine maintaining a constant speed, overtaking a vehicle on the left lane, and returning to the right lane while keeping a safe distance from the passed vehicle. Repeat this exercise 5 times with your eyes closed. Have you done it? Now, still with your eyes closed, repeat the first exercise and add searching for the passed vehicle in the rearview mirror.

Second Exercise highway overtaking return to the right lane.

Ready, set, go: Close your eyes and, while remaining relaxed, mentally imagine maintaining a constant speed, overtaking a vehicle on the left lane, searching for the passed vehicle in the rearview mirror, and signaling with the right turn signal to return to the right lane. Repeat this exercise 5 times with your eyes closed. Have you done it? Now, still with your eyes closed, repeat the second exercise and add looking for the dynamic arrival point on the right lane.

Third Exercise highway overtaking return to the right lane.

Ready, set, go: Close your eyes and, while remaining relaxed, mentally imagine maintaining a constant speed, overtaking a vehicle on the left lane, searching for the passed vehicle in the rearview mirror, signaling with the right turn signal to return to the right lane, and looking for the dynamic arrival point on the right lane. Repeat this exercise 5 times with your eyes closed. Have you done it? Now, still with your eyes closed, repeat the third exercise and add searching for the dynamic endpoint on the right lane.

Fourth Exercise: Overtaking on the highway and returning to the right lane.

Ready, set, go: Close your eyes and, relaxed, imagine: Maintaining a constant speed. Looking for the vehicle overtaken in the central rearview mirror. Activating the right turn signal. Looking for the dynamic endpoint on the right lane. Reaching the dynamic endpoint. Turning off the turn signal. Repeat this exercise 5 times always with your eyes closed. Have you done it? Now, still with your eyes closed, repeat the fourth exercise and add reaching the dynamic endpoint.

Fifth Exercise: Overtaking on the highway and returning to the right lane.

Ready, set, go: Close your eyes and, relaxed, imagine: Maintaining a constant speed. Looking for the vehicle overtaken in the central rearview mirror. Activating the right turn signal. Looking for the dynamic endpoint on the right lane. Reaching the dynamic endpoint. Turning off the turn signal. Repeat this exercise 5 times always with your eyes closed. Have you done it? Now, still with your eyes closed, repeat the fifth exercise and add or remove the turn signal.

Sixth Exercise: Overtaking on the highway and returning to the right lane.

Ready, set, go: Close your eyes and, relaxed, imagine: Maintaining a constant speed. Looking for the vehicle overtaken in the central rearview mirror. Activating the right turn signal. Looking for the dynamic endpoint on the right lane. Reaching the dynamic endpoint. Turning off the turn signal. Repeat this exercise 5 times always with your eyes closed. Have you done it? Now, to make the overtaking and returning to the right lane exercise automatic, close your eyes and visualize the road where you are doing the exercise. Repeat the exercise 14 times. Are you ready? Maintaining a constant speed. Looking for the vehicle overtaken in the central rearview mirror. Activating the right turn signal. Looking for the dynamic endpoint on the right lane. Reaching the dynamic endpoint. Turning off the turn signal. Your brain has recorded everything in such a way that you no longer have to think about these 6 elements, while keeping intact the 7 elements used by your consciousness.

Crosswalks and pedestrians.

I have some questions for you:

What should I know about pedestrians in road traffic? Answer: Pedestrians, who also represent ourselves, always have the right of way over everyone else. There are particularly vulnerable pedestrians such as children, temporarily disabled individuals, permanently disabled individuals, and the elderly who require special attention.

Should pedestrians be given priority? Answer: Pedestrians should be given priority when they have the right of way, and when they are in difficulty even if they do not have the right of way.

How far away from crosswalks can I park in the absence of prohibitions? Answer: 10 meters.

Now let's begin with the visualization learning technique for pedestrians.

First Pedestrian Exercise.

Ready, set, go:
Close your eyes and, while remaining relaxed, mentally imagine:
Looking for the signal, pedestrians and waiting for them. Repeat this exercise 5 times with your eyes closed. Have you done it? Now, still with your eyes closed, repeat the first exercise and add: Adapt your speed to allow for the three possibilities (go, slow down and stop).

Second Pedestrian Exercise.

Ready, set, go: Close your eyes and, while remaining relaxed, mentally imagine:
Looking for the signal, pedestrians and waiting for them. Adapt your speed to allow for the three possibilities (go, slow down and stop). Repeat this exercise 5 times with your eyes closed. Have you done it? Now, still with your eyes closed, repeat the second exercise and add: If the pedestrian is about 1 meter from the crossing, stop to let them pass.

Third Pedestrian Exercise.

Ready, set, go: Close your eyes and, while remaining relaxed, mentally imagine:
Looking for the signal, pedestrians and waiting for them. Adapt your speed to allow for the three possibilities (go, slow down and stop). If the pedestrian is about 1 meter from the crossing, stop to let them pass. Repeat this exercise 5 times with your eyes closed. Have you done it?

Repeat the exercise twice with the variation: slow down and go (the space has cleared before you have to stop), go when there are no pedestrians. Make the pedestrian crossings and pedestrians stopping exercise automatic. Close your eyes and visualize the road where you will do the exercise. Repeat it 14 times. Are you ready? Look for the signal, the pedestrians and wait for them. Adapt your speed so that you can go, slow down and stop. Stop if the pedestrian is about 1 meter from the pedestrian crossing. Make the pedestrian crossings and pedestrians stopping exercise automatic, slow down and go. Close your eyes and visualize the road where you will do the exercise. Repeat it 14 times. Are you ready? Look for the signal, the pedestrians and wait for them. Adapt your speed so that you can go, slow down and stop. Go if the pedestrian has just crossed and cleared the space. Make the pedestrian crossings and pedestrians stopping exercise automatic, go. Close your eyes and visualize the road where you will do the exercise. Repeat it 14 times. Are you ready?

Look for the signal, the pedestrians and wait for them. Adapt your speed so that you can go, slow down and stop. Go if there are no pedestrians and the space is clear. Your brain has recorded everything so that you won't have to think about these 6 elements anymore, while keeping the 7 elements used by your consciousness intact.

1. List of the exercises you have performed:
2. There are three steps to consider:
3. First Exercise: left turn.
4. First Exercise: right turn.
5. Pre-selection to the right:
6. Pre-selection to the left:
7. Exercise Right-hand preselection:
8. Exercise Left-hand preselection:
9. First exercise: left lane change in a one-way street.
10. Make the left automatic preselection.
11. Let's examine the three options in roundabouts:
12. First exercise for the roundabout:
13. Repeat the exercise for the second option, slowing down and going.
14. Repeat the exercise for the third option, stopping.
15. Giving way to the right applies everywhere.
16. Stop:
17. Right-of-Way
18. First Exercise Right-of-Way
19. Right-of-Way Exercise One:

20. Making the right-of-way exercise automatic. Let's do it.
21. Give right-of-way to straight traffic.Stop
22. First Exercise for giving way straight ahead:
23. Option 1
24. Option 2
25. Option 3
26. Making the exercise of giving way while turning right automatic.
27. "Go"
28. "Slow down and go"
29. "Stop"
30. First exercise: give way by turning left. Stop.
31. Let's start with the technique of learning through visualization for straight stops.
32. First exercise: straight stop with free space.
33. Make the straight stop exercise automatic.
34. First exercise: straight stop with occupied space.
35. First exercise right stop with preselection.
36. First exercise - left turn with preselection:
37. Exercise 18: Make the Stop exercise automatic,
38. making the right turn with preselection.
39. First exercise: Traveling on the right lane in the city.
40. First exercise for changing lanes from left to right in the city.
41. Fifth Exercise lane change from the left to the right in the city.
42. Changing Lanes in a Roundabout.
43. Can everyone go on the highway?
44. Let's start with the technique of learning through visualization
45. for entering the highway from the acceleration lane.
46. Exercise 24: Automatic highway entry.
47. Highway exit
48. 25 - Making the highway exit exercise automatic.

49. Safe distance:
50. First exercise, overtaking on the highway and returning to the right lane.
51. Crosswalks and pedestrians.
52. First Pedestrian Exercise.